Whimsical Cats
COLORING BOOK

ANGELA PORTER

DOVER PUBLICATIONS
GARDEN CITY, NEW YORK

Feline fans will enjoy coloring these thirty-one *purr*fectly delightful illustrations created by Angela Porter in her fanciful and fun style. The playful pictures include cats napping, stretching, squeezing into tight spaces, and even riding in a hot-air balloon! The images are printed on one side only, and the pages are perforated for easy removal and display of your finished artwork.

Bibliographical Note

Whimsical Cats Coloring Book is a new work,
first published by Dover Publications in 2022.

International Standard Book Number

ISBN-13: 978-0-486-84866-2
ISBN-10: 0-486-84866-3

Manufactured in the United States of America
84866302
www.doverpublications.com